This book was made in collaboration with Peter Appel Transport

More titles in this series:

With thanks to Ron Niens, Remco Hogenbirk, and Loïc Daems

Copyright © 2023 Clavis Publishing Inc., New York

Originally published as *De vrachtwagenchauffeur*
in Belgium and the Netherlands by Clavis Uitgeverij, 2018
English translation from the Dutch by Clavis Publishing Inc., New York

Visit us on the Web at www.clavis-publishing.com.

Truck Drivers and What They Do written and illustrated by Liesbet Slegers

ISBN 978-1-60537-860-2

This book was printed in January 2023 at Nikara, M. R. Štefánika 858/25, 963 01 Krupina, Slovakia.

First Edition
10 9 8 7 6 5 4 3 2 1

Clavis Publishing supports the First Amendment and celebrates the right to read.

Truck Drivers
and What They Do

Liesbet Slegers

Clavis

NEW YORK

Take a look around you. From furniture and toilet paper to bread and fruit, almost everything you see was transported in a truck. And it's the truck driver who takes care of loading, transporting, and unloading all those things.

With a safety vest on, the driver can get out of the truck in dangerous places.

The truck driver wears useful clothes. Sturdy safety boots and work gloves are handy during loading and unloading. Sunglasses can help against the bright sunlight on the road. When the truck driver loads or unloads cold food like ice cream, he wears a freezer suit to stay warm. Of course, a girl can become a truck driver too!

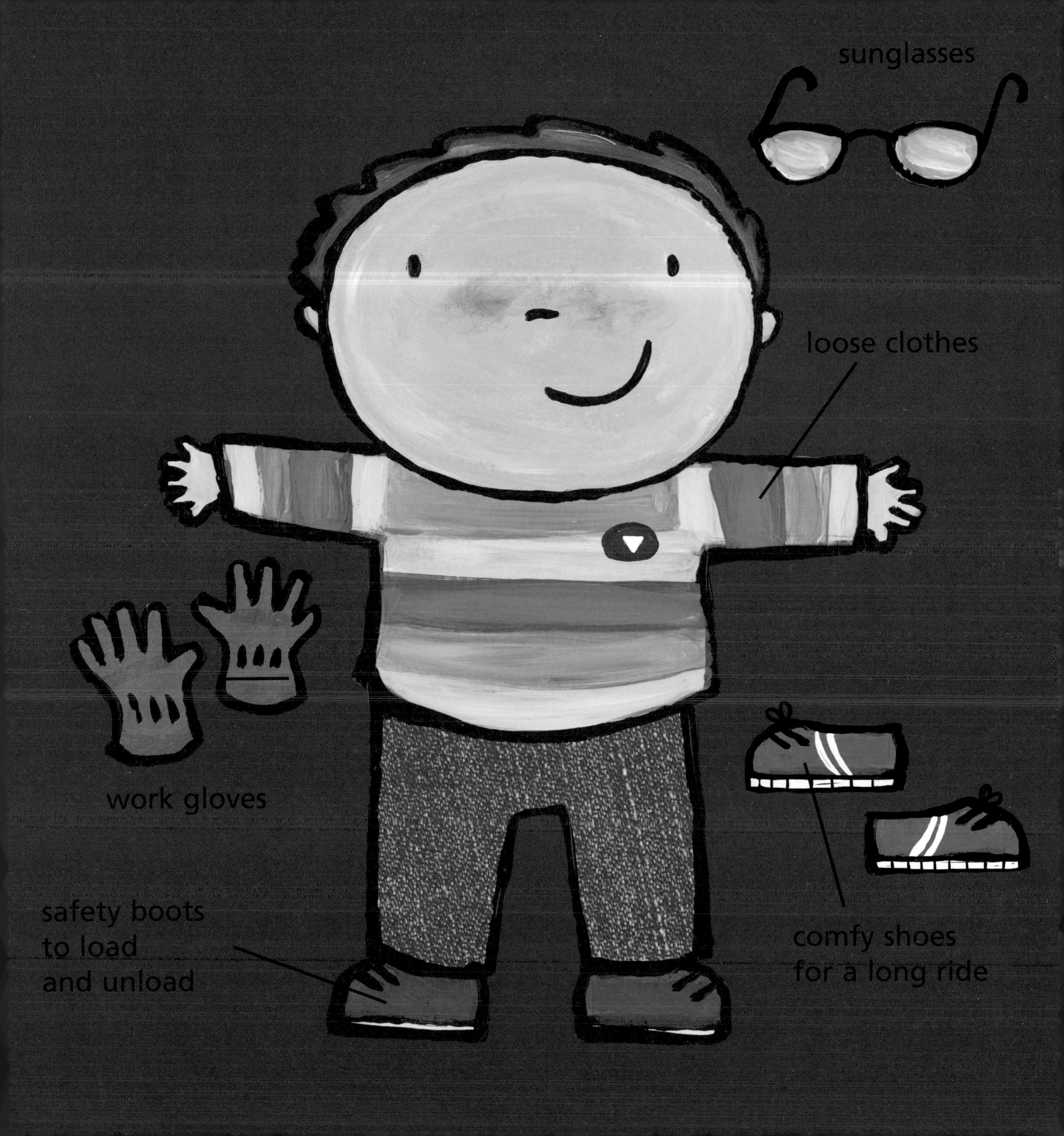

sunglasses

loose clothes

work gloves

safety boots
to load
and unload

comfy shoes
for a long ride

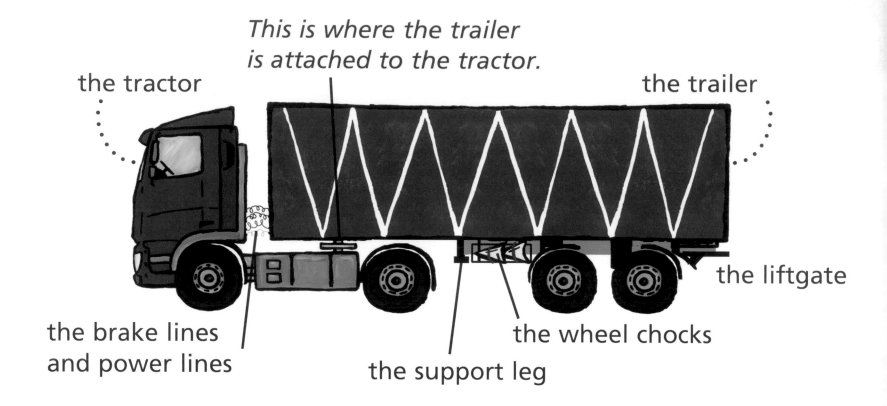

This is where the trailer is attached to the tractor.

the tractor

the trailer

the liftgate

the brake lines and power lines

the wheel chocks

the support leg

What are the different parts of a truck? In the front is the **tractor** with the **cabin**, or cab, where the driver sits. It has a mini-fridge and often a bed. The driver uses a **CB radio** to talk to other drivers. The **tachograph** tracks his hours and tells him when to take breaks. With an **onboard computer**, he can keep in touch with his clients. A **GPS system** shows the driver which way to go. Behind the **tractor** is the **trailer**, which contains the cargo. **Straps** and **load bars** keep everything in place. With **support legs** and **wheel chocks**, the trailer can be separated from the tractor and stand on its own.

in the cabin

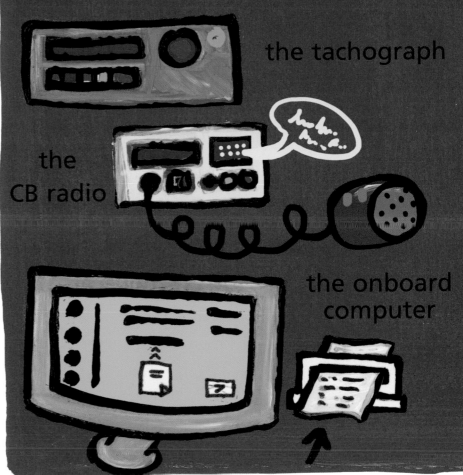

the tachograph

the
CB radio

the onboard
computer

Ice cream is kept very cold.

the strap

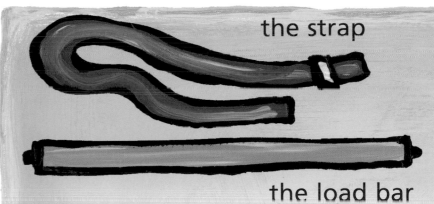

the load bar

the cooling system

It's evening. The truck driver gets his assignments for the next day. He maps out the routes he's going to drive. What's the shortest way? Where will there be less traffic? Which cargo should he transport first? Then he checks the truck. Is the cargo carefully secured? Is the gas tank full? Do the tires all have air? Next he cleans the windows and the rearview mirrors. And the cabin must also be neat. There! The truck is ready to go.

The truck driver goes to bed right after dinner, because tomorrow morning he has to get up very early, when the moon is still high in the sky! He leaves after a cup of coffee and a sandwich. His dog barks happily after him. "Safe journey!" his wife calls out. She can sleep a little longer before she leaves for work. The truck driver puts his food in the fridge of the cabin. He turns on the onboard computer and the tachograph. Then he starts the engine. *Vrrrrrrooooomm!* And now, on to his first stop!

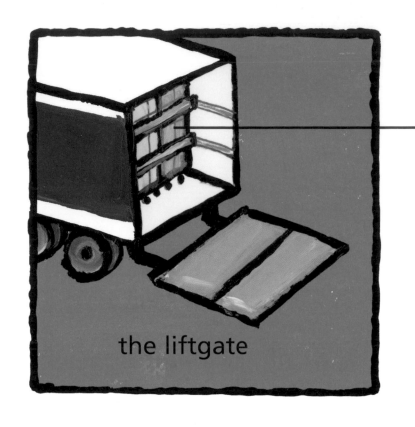

The cargo is well secured with load bars.

the liftgate

After a while, the driver arrives at the distribution center. That's a big warehouse that sends everything to the right stores. "Hello, truck driver! We were expecting you!" says a worker. She loads cold foods like cheese, fruit, meat, and vegetables into the trailer. The driver helps her. He secures the cargo so that nothing moves during the ride. Very clever! Then he sets the correct temperature on the cooling system. This keeps all the food in the trailer cold and fresh. Ready! The truck driver drives off to his next stop.

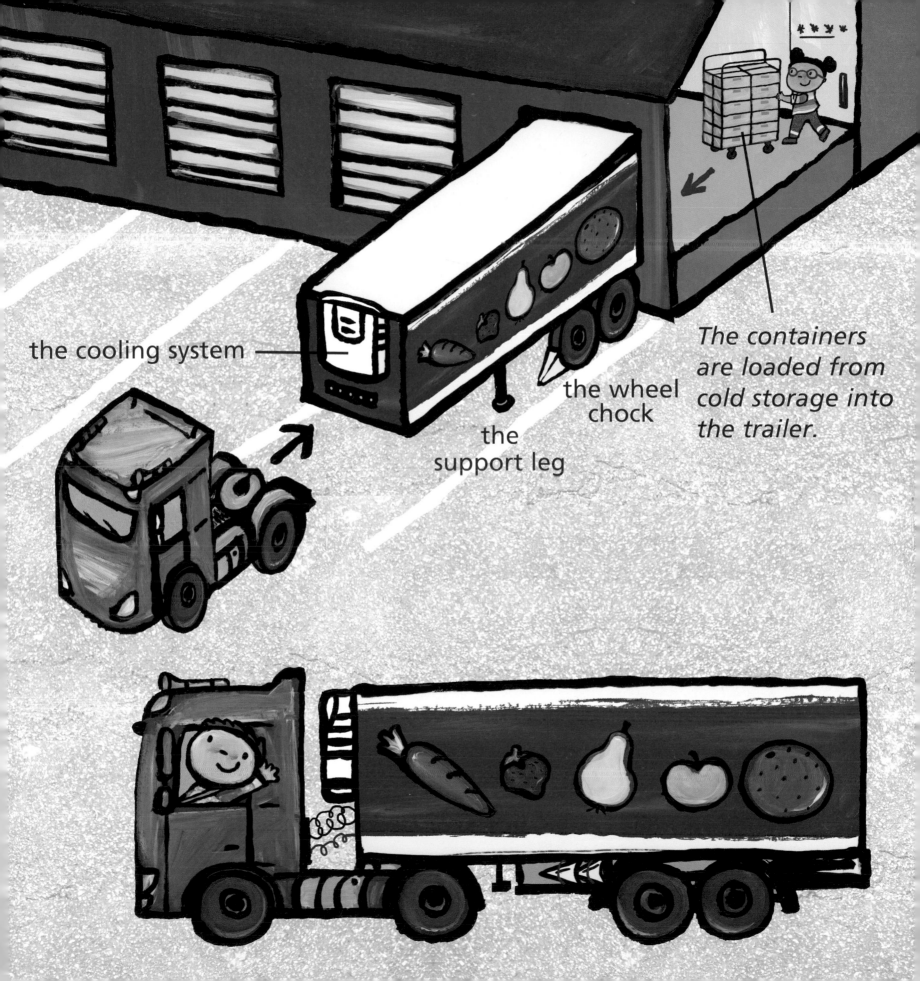

the cooling system

the wheel chock

the support leg

The containers are loaded from cold storage into the trailer.

The truck driver has been driving for an hour. Then it starts to rain hard. Oh dear, the traffic slows down . . . the rain is making it hard for everyone to see. The driver sees the traffic jam on his GPS. What bad luck! Thanks to the CB radio, the truck driver can talk to another driver farther ahead. Is the traffic any better where she is? Our driver hopes he won't arrive late at the store, so that he can finish all his deliveries today before closing time.

A heavy pallet full of boxes is moved with a forklift.

Great! The traffic jam is over. The truck driver arrives at the supermarket. He unloads the containers to carry them inside. Someone from the supermarket signs the order form to confirm that the goods were delivered. Other workers put the food in the store's refrigerators. Now there will be ice cream, fish, yogurt, and other delicious cold food for the store's customers! The truck driver takes back crates that can be refilled and used again.

The driver has packed everything neatly to make good use of the space.

The driver lowers the liftgate.

Empty crates go back.

the gas tank

The truck driver is leaving again. He stops at a restaurant along the highway for a break. He also refuels his truck, because the gas tank is almost empty. It's nice to meet other drivers here, like Mary and Will. After a cup of coffee, our truck driver makes his last stop of the day. When the truck is empty, he shuts down the cooling system and drives back to the distribution center. He turns in the order forms and the empty containers. Then he disconnects the trailer. The working day is over, and the truck driver can go home!

Mary stays in the roadside restaurant. She uses one of the showers, which were built especially for truck drivers. A shower feels good when you're on the road for more than one day. Then she goes to sleep for several hours in the cabin. It's quite cozy with curtains, books, and a warm blanket. Tonight, she drives on again, to a new destination. She likes driving at night.

Mary slept well. She's ready for another trip. There are large headlights above the windshield of her truck to help her drive in the dark. She has to be extra careful, because there are two trailers attached to her truck, one after the other. Driving is even better with some nice music on! Every now and then she stops to rest. She keeps track of her hours with the tachograph. That way, the police can check whether a truck driver is resting enough. That's good!

After a night of driving, Mary arrives at a large distribution center by the ocean. She'll unload her cargo there. Then it will be put on a ship to go someplace else. It's almost morning. The distribution center will open in an hour. Mary has time to enjoy a drink from her fridge in the cabin and to look at the sunrise.

Truck drivers have a lot of freedom, and they enjoy it! They sometimes drive in busy traffic, but they also get to drive to beautiful places: by the ocean, in the forest, and in the mountains. Would you also like to become a truck driver? *Toot, toot!*

There are lots of different trucks. Have you seen this kind before?

transporting hazardous materials

These signs tell you that there are dangerous substances on board.

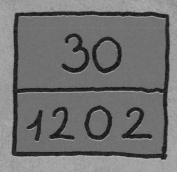  

There's a code on the **orange** sign. That way, emergency responders immediately know what's in the tank in case of an accident.

The **red** sign shows a flame. That means the substance in the tank can catch on fire. Be careful!

The **white** sign makes it clear that the substances in the tank are dangerous for nature.